THIS NOTEBOOK BELONGS TO

____

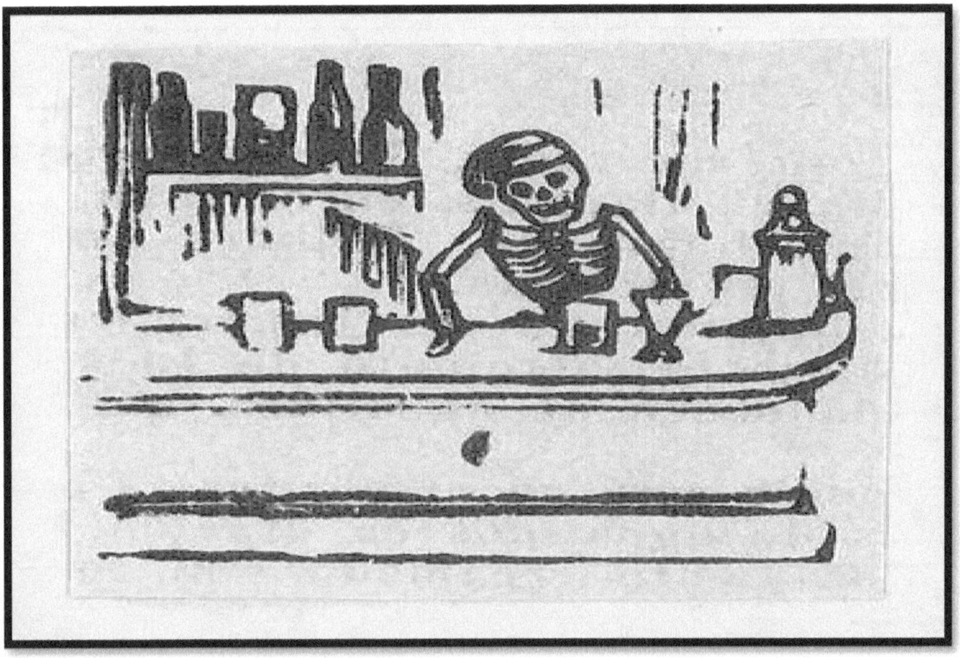

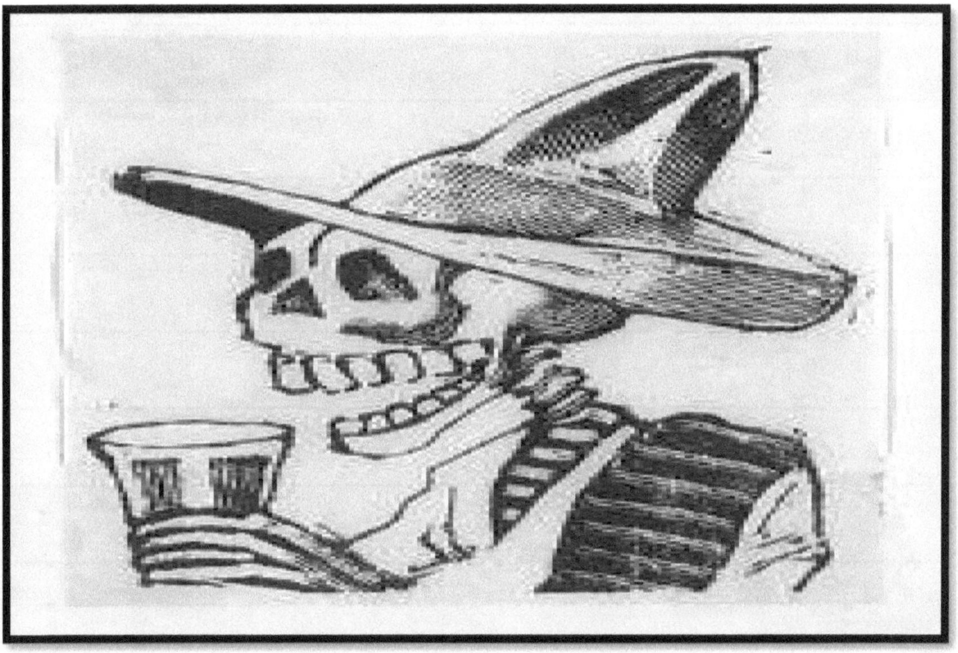

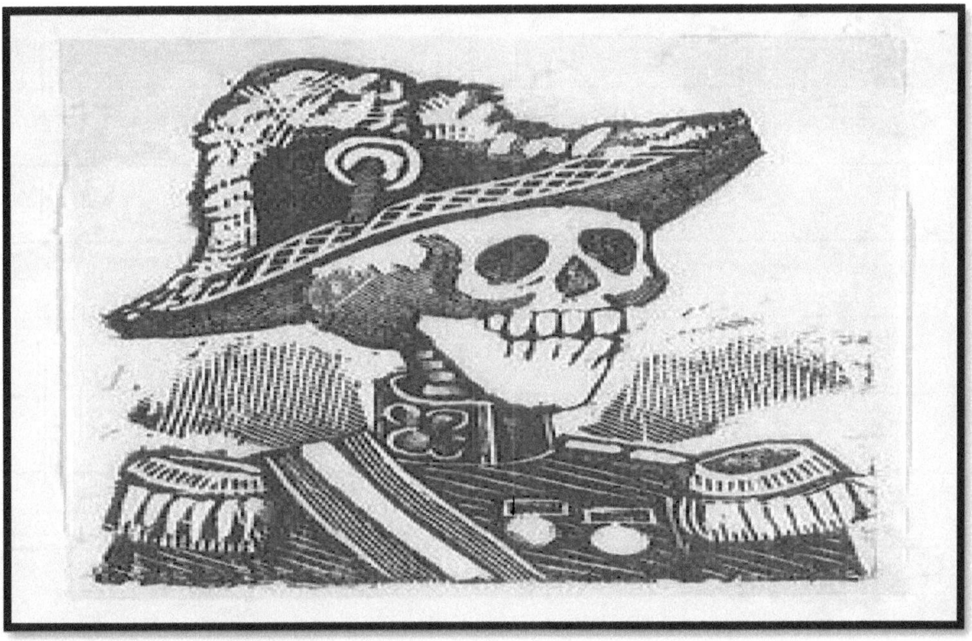

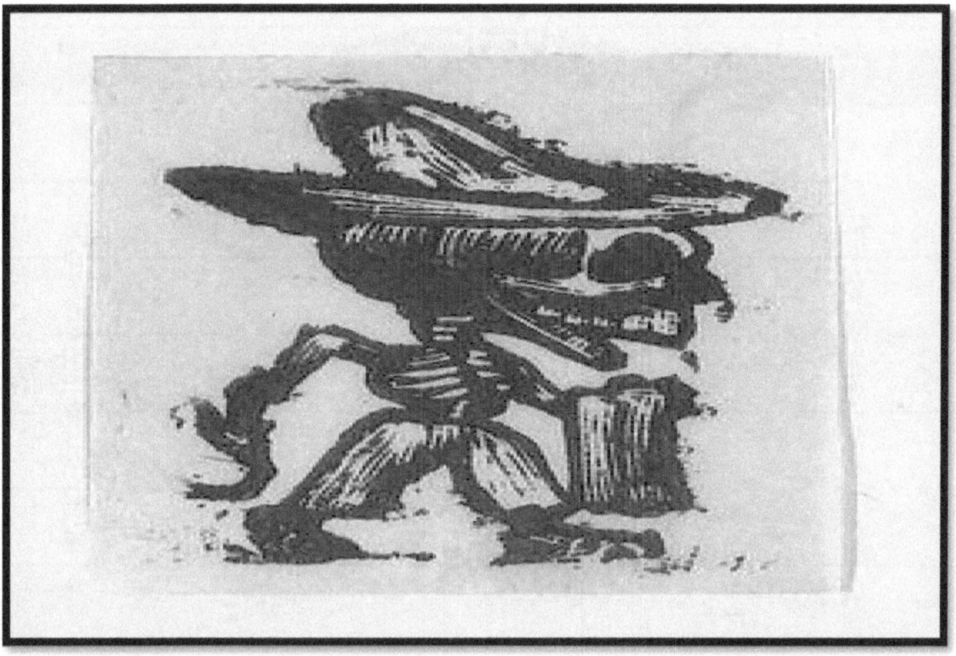

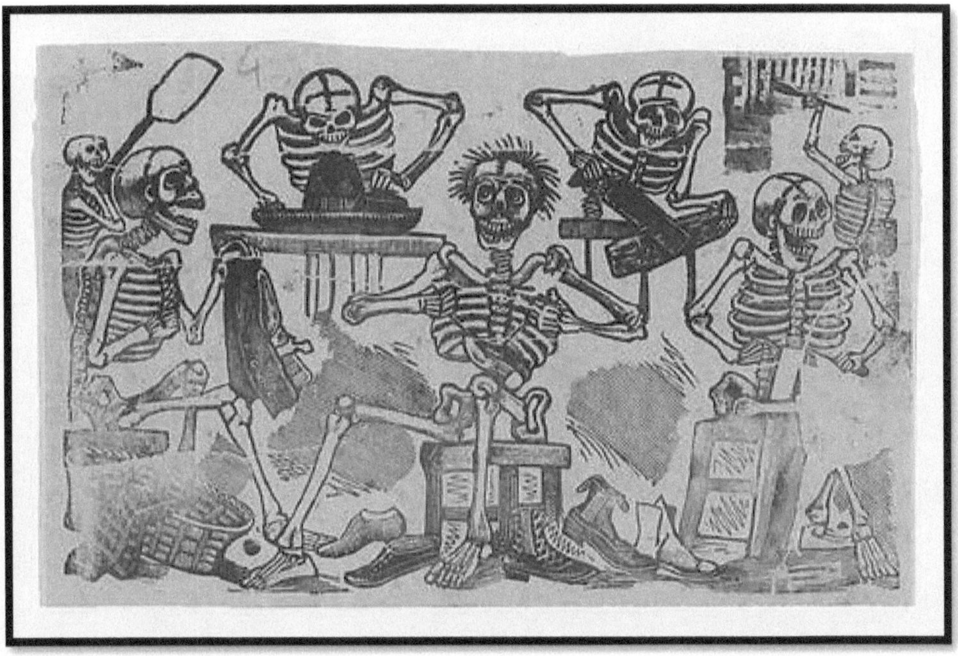

www.ingramcontent.com/pod-product-compliance
Lightning Source LLC
Chambersburg PA
CBHW030945240526
45463CB00016B/1957
9781696300674